As Expounded by Dada Bhagwan

Noble Use of Money

Originally Compiled in Gujarati by:
Dr. Niruben Amin

Publisher	: Mr. Ajit C. Patel
Dada Bhagwan Vignan Foundation
1, Varun Apartment, 37, Shrimali Society,
Opp. Navrangpura Police Station,
Navrangpura, Ahmedabad: 380009.
Gujarat, India.
Tel. : +91 79 35002100, +91 9328661166-77
©	**Dada Bhagwan Foundation**
5, Mamta Park Society, B\h. Navgujarat College,
Usmanpura, Ahmedabad - 380014, Gujarat, India.
Email: info@dadabhagwan.org Tel.: +91 9328661166-77
All Rights Reserved. No part of this publication may be shared, copied, translated or reproduced in any form (including electronic storage or audio recording) without written permission from the holder of the copyright.
This publication is licensed for your personal use only.

1st Edition	:	2,000 copies,	March 2006
2nd to 4th Edition	:	9000 copies,	June 2007 to November 2016
5th Edition	:	2000 copies,	June 2021

Price	: Ultimate humility and the intent that 'I do not know anything'!
Rs. 30.00

Printer	: Amba Multiprint
B - 99, Electronics GIDC, K-6 Road,
Sector - 25, Gandhinagar-382044.
Gujarat, India.
Tel. : +91 79 35002142, +91 9328660055

ISBN/eISBN : 978-93-86289-10-0

Printed in India

Trimantra

The Three Mantras That Destroy All Obstacles in Life

Namo Vitaraagaya
I bow to the Ones who are absolutely free from all attachment and abhorrence

Namo Arihantanam
I bow to the living Ones who have annihilated all internal enemies of anger, pride, deceit and greed

Namo Siddhanam
I bow to the Ones who have attained the state of total and final liberation

Namo Aayariyanam
I bow to the Self-realized masters who impart the Knowledge of the Self to others

Namo Uvazzayanam
I bow to the Ones who have received the Knowledge of the Self and are helping others attain the same

Namo Loye Savva Sahunam
I bow to the Ones, wherever they may be, who have received the Knowledge of the Self

Eso Pancha Namukkaro
These five salutations

Savva Pavappanasano
Destroy all demerit karma

Mangalanam Cha Savvesim
Of all that is auspicious

Padhamam Havai Mangalam ‖1‖
This is the highest

Om Namo Bhagavate Vasudevaya ‖2‖
I bow to the Ones who have attained the absolute Self in human form

Om Namah Shivaya ‖3‖
I bow to all human beings who have become instruments for the salvation of the world

Jai Sat Chit Anand
Awareness of the Eternal is Bliss

Who Is Dada Bhagwan?

In June 1958, around 6 o'clock one evening, amidst the hustle and bustle of the Surat railway station while seated on a bench, 'Dada Bhagwan' manifested completely within the sacred bodily form of Ambalal Muljibhai Patel. Nature revealed a remarkable phenomenon of spirituality! In the span of an hour, the vision of the universe was unveiled to him! Complete clarity for all spiritual questions such as, 'Who are we? Who is God? Who runs the world? What is karma? What is liberation?' etc. was attained.

What He attained that evening, He imparted to others through his original Scientific experiment (*Gnan Vidhi*) in just two hours! This has been referred to as the *Akram* path. *Kram* means to climb up sequentially, step-by-step while *Akram* means step-less, a shortcut, the elevator path!

He, himself, would explain to others who Dada Bhagwan is by saying, "The one visible before you is not Dada Bhagwan. I am the *Gnani Purush* and the One who has manifested within is Dada Bhagwan who is the Lord of the fourteen worlds. He is also within you, and within everyone else too. He resides unmanifest within you, whereas here [within A. M. Patel], He has manifested completely! I, myself, am not God (*Bhagwan*); I also bow down to the Dada Bhagwan who has manifest within me."

❖ ❖ ❖ ❖ ❖

The Current Link to Attain Self-Realization

After attaining the Knowledge of the Self in 1958, absolutely revered Dada Bhagwan (Dadashri) traveled nationally and internationally to impart spiritual discourse and Self-realization to spiritual seekers.

During his lifetime itself, Dadashri had given the spiritual power to Pujya Dr. Niruben Amin (Niruma) to bestow Self-realization to others. In the same way, after Dadashri left his mortal body, Pujya Niruma conducted spiritual discourses (*satsang*) and imparted Self-realization to spiritual seekers, as an instrumental doer. Dadashri had also given Pujya Deepakbhai Desai the spiritual power to conduct *satsang*. At present, with the blessings of Pujya Niruma, Pujya Deepakbhai travels nationally and internationally to impart Self-realization as an instrumental doer.

After Self-realization, thousands of spiritual seekers prevail in a state free from bondage and dwell in the experience of the Self, whilst carrying out all their worldly responsibilities.

❖ ❖ ❖ ❖ ❖

Note About This Translation

The *Gnani Purush*, Ambalal M. Patel, also commonly known as 'Dadashri' or 'Dada', gave spiritual discourses that were in the form of answers to questions asked by spiritual aspirants. These discourses were recorded and compiled into books by Pujya Dr. Niruben Amin in the Gujarati language.

Dadashri had said that it would be impossible to translate His *satsangs* and the Knowledge about the Science of Self-realization word for word into other languages, because some of the meaning would be lost in the process. Therefore, in order to understand precisely the *Akram* Science of Self-realization, He stressed the importance of learning Gujarati.

However, Dadashri did grant His blessings to translate His words into other languages so that spiritual seekers could benefit to a certain degree and later progress through their own efforts. This book is not a literal translation, but great care has been taken to preserve the essence of His original message.

Spiritual discourses have been and continue to be translated from Gujarati. For certain Gujarati words, several translated words or even sentences are needed to convey the meaning, hence many Gujarati words have been retained within the translated text for better understanding. Where the Gujarati word is used for the first time, it is italicized, followed by a translation explaining its meaning in parenthesis. Subsequently, only the Gujarati word is used in the text that follows. This serves a two-fold benefit; firstly, ease of translation and reading, and secondly, make the reader more familiar with the Gujarati words, which is critical for a deeper understanding of this spiritual Science. The content in square brackets provides further clarity regarding the matter, which is not present in the original Gujarati content.

This is a humble attempt to present to the world, the essence of His Knowledge. While reading this translation, if there is any contradiction or discrepancy, then it is the mistake of the translators and the understanding of the matter should be clarified with the living *Gnani* to avoid misinterpretation.

❖ ❖ ❖ ❖ ❖

Special Note to the Reader

The Self is the Soul (*Atma*) within all living beings.

The term pure Soul is used by the *Gnani Purush* for the awakened Self, after the *Gnan Vidhi*. The word Self, with an uppercase 'S', refers to the awakened Self which is separate from the worldly-interacting self, which is written with a lowercase 's'.

Wherever Dadashri uses the term 'we', 'us', or 'our', He is referring to Himself, the *Gnani Purush*.

Similarly, the use of You or Your in the middle of a sentence, with an uppercase first letter, or 'You', 'Your' in single quotes at the beginning of the sentence, refers to the state of the awakened Self or *Pragnya*. This is an important distinction for the correct understanding of the difference between the awakened Self and the worldly-interacting self.

Wherever the name 'Chandubhai' is used, the reader should substitute his or her name and read the matter accordingly.

The masculine third person pronoun 'he' and likewise the object pronoun 'him' have been used for the most part throughout the translation. Needless to say, 'he' includes 'she' and 'him' includes 'her'.

For reference, a glossary of all the Gujarati words is either provided at the back of this book or available on our website at:

http://www.dadabhagwan.org/books-media/glossary/

❖ ❖ ❖ ❖ ❖

Editorial

Scriptures and religious leaders have described various ways to bind merit karma (*punya*). One of those ways is by giving donation (*daan*). To give donation means to give happiness to others by giving them something that belongs to oneself.

The practice of giving donation is inculcated in people at an early age. Hence, even when a small child is taken to the temple, he is taught to give money and food to the needy people who sit outside the temple; he is taught to put money in the collection box in the temple. In this way, donating is instilled as a value from childhood.

Absolutely revered Dadashri has explained the subtleties of how one can even incur a tremendous loss if there is a lack of awareness within at the time of making a donation. What kind of awareness should one maintain while giving a donation? What is the best donation? What are the various types of donation? What kind of intentions should be behind it? To whom can a donation be given? Extensive information on this and various other details about giving donation which have been expressed in Dadashri's Knowledge-laden speech, have been compiled and published in this booklet. For the reader, this will become an ultimate guide on giving donation!

-**Dr. Niruben Amin**

❖ ❖ ❖ ❖ ❖

Noble Use of Money

Why Give a Donation?

Questioner: Why do people give donations (*daan*)?

Dadashri: The truth is, one gives a donation because he wants something in return. He gives happiness in order to get happiness in return. He doesn't donate for the purpose of liberation (*moksha*). If you give happiness to people, then you will get happiness in return. Whatever you give, you will get in return. So this is the law. We receive by giving to others. By taking away from others, we inevitably end up losing it.

Questioner: Is it better to fast or is it better to make a donation?

Dadashri: To make a donation means to sow seeds in a field. When seeds are sown in a field, they will give result. And by fasting, the [spiritual] awareness will increase internally. However, the Lord has said to fast according to one's own capability.

To Give a Donation Means to Give Happiness

To give a donation means to give happiness to any other living being, be it humans or any other animals. That is called *daan*. And when you give happiness to others, in its reaction, you will get only happiness. If you give happiness, then happiness immediately comes to you without any effort!

When you donate, you will feel happiness within. You are giving away your own money, yet you feel happy, because you are doing something good. When you do a good deed, you feel happy, and when you do a bad deed, you feel misery. Based on this, are you able to identify which of the two is good and which one is bad?

The Way to Attain Bliss

Questioner: In order to attain peace of mind, should we serve those who are poor, those who are weak, or should we worship God or should we give a donation to someone? What should we do?

Dadashri: If you want peace of mind, then you should feed others what belongs to you. Bring a large container of ice cream tomorrow and feed all these people. Then tell me how much happiness you feel at that time. These people don't want to eat ice cream. But just try doing this for your own peace. These people aren't eager to eat ice cream in winter. Similarly, if there are any animals around you, if you throw roasted chickpeas to monkeys, they will delightedly jump up and down, and at that time, your happiness will have no bounds. They will go on eating and your happiness will have no bounds. These pigeons jump about even before you give them grains. And when you give it to them, you are giving away something of your own, so happiness begins to arise within. Suppose a person takes a fall on the road and breaks his leg and there is blood gushing forth; if you tear off a piece of your garment and bandage his leg, then you will feel happiness at that time. It doesn't matter whether your garment was costly; if you tear it and bandage his leg, then you will feel tremendous happiness at that time.

Where Should Donations Be Given?

Questioner: In certain religions, it is said that whatever you earn, you should give a certain percentage of that as a donation, donate five to ten percent of it. So what about that?

Dadashri: There is no problem with giving a donation for religious purposes. But donate to a religious institution where the money is being used in the right way towards religion. Do not donate where it is being misused, donate it elsewhere.

Be completely certain that the money is being used in the right way. Otherwise, if you have surplus money, then it will take you to a lower life-form. So, make sure that money is put to use in a good way in any place. However, religious leaders should not be taking in money [for their personal use].

Direct Your Money Towards Religion

It is very difficult to manage money! It is better to earn less instead. If a person earns ten thousand rupees in twelve months and he donates one thousand for a religious purpose, then he will not have any problems. A person giving hundreds of thousands and this person giving a thousand rupees are both considered equivalent, but one should at least give a thousand rupees. What I am saying is that don't give zilch, give the bare minimum if you don't have much, and if you have more and you direct it towards religion, then you will not incur any liability. Otherwise, there will be a liability. It [excess money] causes a lot of suffering! It is extremely difficult to manage money. It is easier to look after cows and buffalos; if they are tied to a pole, then at least they won't drift away by morning. But it is very difficult to manage money. It is very difficult; it brings about a lot of problems.

For Whom Does Money Not Last?

Questioner: I earn ten thousand rupees per month, but why does my money not last very long?

Dadashri: The money earned after the year 1942 does not last very long. This money is associated with demerit karma (*paap*), that is why it does not last very long. The money that is earned after two to five years from now will last long. Even though 'we' are a *Gnani* (One who has realized the Self and is able to do the same for others), 'we' are earning money, yet it does not last long. There is enough money to pay the income tax, that's it.

Questioner: What should we do as money does not last very long?

Dadashri: Money is not something that lasts very long. But change the direction of its flow. If it is going in a certain direction, then redirect its flow and channel it towards religion. Meaning, however much is spent towards a worthy cause is worthwhile. Once God comes [into your home], then Lakshmiji (the Goddess of wealth; Hindu personification of money) will last; other than that, how would Lakshmiji last? Where God is present, no conflicts will arise, but where Lakshmiji alone is present, there will be conflicts and arguments. People earn a lot of money, but they spend it on useless things. Money can be used for a good cause by someone with tremendous merit karma. When money is used for a good cause, it is considered tremendous merit karma (*punya*).

Money earned after 1942 has no quality at all. These days, money is not being spent in the right place. If it is used in the right place, then it is considered very good.

Money Lasts for Seven Generations!

Questioner: In India, Kasturbhai Lalbhai [an Indian

industrialist and philanthropist, 19 December 1894 – 20 January 1980] has a legacy which may continue for two, three or four generations. It carries forward from his children to his grandchildren. Whereas here, in America, one's legacy may last at most for six to eight years and then it all gets used up. If there is money, it disappears, or if there isn't any money, then one may even end up with money. So what must be the reason for this?

Dadashri: The truth is, the merit karma over there, in India, that merit karma is so sticky that even if one keeps washing it away, it does not leave. And the demerit karma is also so sticky that even if one keeps washing it away, it does not leave. So, whether one is a Vaishnav [a devotee of Lord Krishna] or a Jain, he has bound merit karma so strongly that even if he keeps clearing it away, it does not leave. The wealth of the generous Ramanlal Sheth of Petlad lasted well into the seventh generation. He would keep magnanimously donating money to people without looking at the amount, yet he never ran out of it. He had bound strong, unwavering merit karma. Similarly, one can also bind such solid demerit karma, that the family does not come out of poverty for seven generations to come. They may suffer endless pain. So it can also be excessive and it can also be within bounds.

Here [in America], it does overflow, and then it also simmers down. And then it overflows again. Even after simmering down, it may overflow again. It does not take long here, whereas there, [in India], after simmering down, it takes a very long time for it to overflow again. So there, it would last for seven generations. These days, all the merit karma has decreased. Now what happens over here? Who will be born into Kasturbhai's family? Only one who has tremendous merit karma equivalent to what Kasturbhai has will take birth there. Then, who would be born into that person's home? One who has tremendous merit karma just like him! In this case, it is not Kasturbhai's merit karma that is at work. Another person like him comes into the family, so then it is his merit karma, yet it is referred to as Kasturbhai's legacy. And nowadays, do people with such tremendous merit karma even exist? Recently, in the past twenty-five years, there hasn't been anyone in particular like that.

Otherwise, It Will Go Down the Gutter

In the past, money would last for at least five generations, it would last for at least three generations. These days, money does not last for even one generation. What is the money of the current times like? It does not last for even one generation. This money is such that it comes and leaves in his own presence. This is actually money coming as a result of *paapanubandhi punya* (karmic effect of merit karma of this life, which binds demerit karma for the next life). However little money you have which has come as a result of *punyanubandhi punya* (karmic effect of merit karma in this life, which binds merit karma for the next life), is what inspires you to come here. It brings you here and makes you spend money here. That money gets used for a good cause, otherwise, it will all be squandered away. Everything will go down the gutter. These children are enjoying your money, aren't they? And if you tell them, "You are enjoying my money." Then they will retort, "What do you mean by yours? We are indeed enjoying what is ours." So, it is all going down the gutter, isn't it!

Direct the Flow of Surplus Money Towards Charity

Actually, one learns through societal influence, by observing others. However, if we were to ask the *Gnani*, then He would say, "No, why are you falling into this pit in this way?" One comes out of the pit of miseries, but then he falls into this pit of money. If you have surplus money, then give it to charity. Only that will get credited to your account [as merit karma that will unfold in the next life], whereas this bank balance will not accumulate [carry forward to the next life]. Moreover, you will not face any difficulty. The one who gives to charity does not face difficulties.

Redirect Its Flow

In times of need, only *dharma* (giving happiness to others; maintaining good intentions; rightful action) will help you. Therefore, let the money flow towards *dharma*. Only in *Sushamkaal* (an era of the time cycle characterized predominantly by happiness, and almost no unhappiness) was it worth having illusory attachment (*moha*) for money. That kind of money doesn't come [now]! Who causes heart failure and high blood pressure in these rich businessmen? It is indeed the money of this era of the time cycle.

What is the nature of money? It is transitory. Meaning, it comes and one fine day it leaves. Therefore, use money for the benefit of others. When the unfolding of your karma is unfavorable, only what you had given to others will help you. So you should understand this right from the beginning. Money should indeed be expended appropriately, shouldn't it?

Once your conduct [related to sexuality] becomes pure, you will have won over the entire world. Then go ahead, eat and drink whatever you want, and if you have surplus, feed it to others. What else can you do? Can you take it with you? Only the money you spend on others is yours, that much is the balance for the next life. So if someone wants to accumulate balance for the next life, then he should spend money on others. Then be it for anybody not related to you, be it any living being, even if it's a crow and it samples just a small amount [of food], that will be [credited] in your balance! However, what you and your children ate, that will not be [credited] in your balance, all of that will have gone down the gutter. But you cannot stop it from going down the gutter, you are duty-bound there. So is there any way to break away from this? [No,] But alongside, you should understand that everything that is not used for others indeed goes down the gutter.

If you don't feed human beings, but at least if you feed crows, if you feed sparrows, if you feed all of them, then that too is considered to have been spent for others. The cost of a plate of food for human beings has increased substantially, hasn't it? The cost of a plate of food for sparrows is not very much, is it? But then again, whatever is credited will also be less, won't it?

Because the Intent Has Spoiled in the Mind...

Questioner: For a certain period of time, I used to donate thirty percent of my income to charity, but all of that has stopped. However much I used to donate, I am unable to do so now.

Dadashri: If you really want to do it, then it will inevitably happen even after two years from now! There is no shortage over there. There is plenty of it there. [But] What can be done if the intent has spoiled in your mind?

Should It Be Given Once It Comes or Does It Come if It Is Given?

We were sitting in one man's bungalow and a cyclone came. So the doors started to rattle. So, he told me, "This cyclone has come. Should I close all the doors?" I replied, "Do not close all the doors. Keep one door open for the wind to enter and close all the exit doors. So how much wind will enter? Only if what is filled is emptied out can the wind enter, isn't it? Otherwise, no cyclone of any sort can enter." Then, I made him experience this. So then he told me, "Now it is not coming in." So this is what it is like with a cyclone.

If you create an obstruction towards money, then it will not flow in. However much is filled in will remain as it is. And if you release it from one side, then more will keep coming in. Otherwise, if you keep it obstructed, then the amount will remain the same. This is how money works. Now, it is up to you which path to let it flow down; whether to expend it for your wife and children's enjoyment, or to expend it for [earning] fame, or to expend it for *gnandaan* (donation of knowledge) or to expend it for *annadaan* (donation of food). What you allow it to get expended towards depends upon you. But if you expend it, then more will come. What will happen if you don't expend it? If you expend it, will more not come in? Yes, it will come in.

The Channels in Which the Flow Can Be Directed

Do you know how many types of donation there are? There are four types of donation. The first is *aahaardaan* (donation of food; also known as *annadaan*), the second is *aushadhdaan* (donation of medicine), the third is *gnandaan* (donation of knowledge), and the fourth is *abhaydaan* (being in a state of conduct which does not induce fear in or hurt any living being).

The First Is Aahaardaan

The first type of donation is *annadaan* (donation of food; also known as *aahaardaan*). For this type of donation, it is said that if someone comes to your door and says, "Please give me something to eat, I am hungry," then you should reply, "Have a seat, sit down for a meal. I will serve you some food." That is *aahaardaan*. But those who use their intellect excessively will say, "You might feed this stout person right now, but how will you feed him again in the evening?" To which the Lord says, "Don't be a wise guy like this. This man has fed him, so he will at least live for today. Tomorrow, he will come across someone else who will help him stay alive. You don't have to think about tomorrow. You are not to interfere as to 'What will he do tomorrow?' He will find something tomorrow. You are not to worry about whether or not you will be able to give him food all the time. As he has come to your door, give him whatever you can. At least he can remain alive today, that's enough! Then tomorrow, he may have some other unfolding of karma, you do not need to worry about that."

Questioner: Is *annadaan* considered the best?

Dadashri: *Annadaan* is considered good. But how much *annadaan* can you give? It's not as though people will give it forever. Even if you feed someone one meal, that is more than enough. He will get something else for his next meal. But for today, he has survived with even one meal, hasn't he! Now, even for this, do these people give leftover food or do they prepare new food?

Questioner: They give only the leftover food. It works to their own advantage. Since there is leftover food, what else would they do?

Dadashri: Nevertheless, they are making good use of that, my brother! However, if one prepares new food and serves it, then I would say that it is correct. The *vitaraag* (absolutely detached) Lords must have some laws, right? Or will it do if things carry on baselessly?

Questioner: No, no, how can things carry on baselessly?!

Dadashri: That will not work with the *vitaraag* Lords; it works everywhere else.

Aushadhdaan

And the second is *aushadhdaan* (donation of medicine). It is considered superior to *aahaardaan*. What happens in *aushadhdaan*? Suppose there is a person who is not so well off financially and he becomes sick. He goes to the hospital and says, "Oh, the doctor has prescribed me this medicine, but I don't have the fifty rupees to purchase it. So how can I obtain this medicine?" At that time, you can tell him, "Here are the fifty rupees for the medicine and here's another ten rupees." Or you can bring the medicine from somewhere else and give it to him for free. You can spend the money to buy the medicine and give it to him free of cost. So if he takes this medicine, then the helpless man can live for four to six years. There is more benefit in giving *aushadhdaan* as compared to *annadaan*. Do you understand? Which gives more benefit? Is *annadaan* better or *aushadhdaan*?

Questioner: *Aushadhdaan*.

Dadashri: *Aushadhdaan* is considered more important than *aahaardaan*, because it may even help keep the person alive for two more months. It helps a person live for a longer period of time. It gives him some relief from the sensation of pain.

As it is, women and children in our society naturally give *annadaan* and *aushadhdaan*. This kind of donation doesn't cost too much, but it should be done. If we encounter someone who is needy, if some unhappy person comes to our door, then immediately give him whatever food is available.

Gnandaan Is Even Better

Then, *gnandaan* (donation of knowledge) is said to be even better. *Gnandaan* includes printing books; to print books that give people the right understanding and lead them on the right path, and which lead to their spiritual benefit is considered *gnandaan*. *Gnandaan* leads one to attain a good life-form, a higher life-form, and even liberation (*moksha*).

So the Lord has said that *gnandaan* is the main thing. And where there is no involvement of money, He has talked about *abhaydaan* (being in a state of conduct which does not induce fear in or hurt any living being). For those who are involved in monetary interactions, He has talked about *gnandaan*, and for people who have a mediocre financial condition, for those who are not so well off, He has talked about these two: *aushadhdaan* and *aahaardaan*.

Questioner: But when one has surplus money, that can be donated, can't it?

Dadashri: Donation is the best. Use it to reduce the miseries that others may have, and secondly, use it on the right path. Do *gnandaan* in such a way that it leads people down the right path. In this world, *gnandaan* is outstanding! You can benefit so much from reading one sentence [of this book filled with Knowledge]! Now, if that book were to go into the hands of people, then how much would they benefit!

Questioner: Now I understood it properly.

Dadashri: Yes, so those who have surplus money should primarily do *gnandaan*.

Now, what kind of knowledge should it be? It should be knowledge that helps people. Yes, it should not be for books containing stories about outlaws. With that kind of knowledge, people keep slipping [descending spiritually]. People do get enjoyment when they read such stories, but that makes them descend to a lower life-form.

Abhaydaan Is the Greatest of All

And the fourth is *abhaydaan*. To conduct oneself in

a way that does not trouble or harass any living being is called *abhaydaan*.

Questioner: Please explain more about *abhaydaan*.

Dadashri: *Abhaydaan* means no living being is hurt by us. I will give you an example. I used to go to the movies when I was young, when I was twenty-two or twenty-five years old. It would be midnight or half past twelve by the time I would return home. As I would come walking, my shoes would make some noise. Because I had metal cleats placed on the soles of my shoes, they would click, and they would make a lot of noise at night. The poor dogs would be sleeping at night, they would be sleeping peacefully, and then they would raise up their ears like this. So, I would understand, 'The poor thing has become startled because of me! What kind of a person am I in this locality that these dogs are becoming startled by me?' So while I was still at a distance, I would remove my shoes beforehand, and I would walk with the shoes in my hands. I would sneak past them, but I would not let them get startled. This was my approach at a young age. They would get startled because of me, wouldn't they?!

Questioner: Yes, it would also disturb their sleep, wouldn't it?

Dadashri: Yes, moreover, they would get startled, and they don't abandon their nature. They would even bark sometimes; it is in their nature. Instead, wouldn't it be better to just let them sleep? That too, they would not bark at those who would live in that locality.

So for *abhaydaan*, first maintain the intent (*bhaav*) that, 'May no living being be hurt in the slightest,' and then it will come into practice. If the intent has been done, then it will come into practice, but what if the intent has not been done at all? Therefore, the Lord has referred to this donation as one that is paramount. There is no need for money in this. This is the highest type of donation of all, but people do not have the capacity for this. Even those who have money are unable to do this. Therefore, those who have money should give donation through money.

So, there is no other type of donation except these four; that is what the Lord has said. The donations that others talk about are of their imagination; [in reality,] there are only these four types of donations. *Aahaardaan, aushadhdaan,* then comes *gnandaan* and *abhaydaan*. As much as possible, maintain the intention to give *abhaydaan*.

Questioner: But do all the other three originate from *abhaydaan*? From this intent?

Dadashri: No. The fact is, *abhaydaan* is something that can be given by a highly [spiritually] developed person. Even an ordinary person, one who doesn't have any money, can give it. Highly [spiritually] developed people may or may not have money. So, they may not have any monetary dealings, but they can definitely give *abhaydaan*. In the past, wealthy men used to give *abhaydaan*, but they cannot do so nowadays; they fall short. They have earned only money, and that too, by instilling fear in people!

Questioner: Have they donated fear?

Dadashri: No, you cannot say such a thing. Even after doing that, they are still spending for *gnandaan*, aren't they? No matter what he has done before coming here, at least he is now spending on *gnandaan*, that is the best thing; that is what the Lord has said.

Only the Gnanis Can Give This Donation

So the best donation is *abhaydaan*. The second best is *gnandaan*. The Lord has praised *abhaydaan*. First, give *abhaydaan* such that no one is afraid of you. The second is *gnandaan*. The third is *aushadhdaan*, and the fourth is *aahaardaan*.

Abhaydaan is superior to *gnandaan*! However, people cannot give *abhaydaan*, can they? Only the *Gnanis* can give *abhaydaan*. The *Gnanis* and the *Gnanis'* family [*mahatmas*; Self-realized Ones] can give *abhaydaan*. The followers of the *Gnani* can give *abhaydaan*. They live in a way that does not incite fear in anyone. They conduct themselves in a way that others around them remain free from fear. Their conduct is such that they would not startle even a dog. This is because the hurt caused to others reaches one's own self. The hurt caused to others reaches one's own self; thus, we should live in such a way that we do not cause the slightest fear in any living being.

Money Is Involved in All Three

Questioner: Then is there no scope for the donation of money?

Dadashri: The donation of money is covered by *gnandaan*. If you get some books printed right now, then money is involved in that; that is *gnandaan*.

Questioner: Everything indeed happens through the means of money, doesn't it? Even *annadaan* is given through the means of money, isn't it?

Dadashri: Even when you want to give medicine, you have to buy it for one hundred rupees and then you can give it to the person in need, right? So, money is inevitably used for everything. However, it is best if money is donated in this way.

How Can It Be Given?

Questioner: So this means, money is not given directly in [the different types of] donations.

Dadashri: Yes, nor should you give it directly. Give it in the form of *gnandaan*, meaning get books printed and distribute those, or provide food by giving prepared meals. Nowhere is it mentioned to donate money directly.

The Donation of Gold Coins

Questioner: In our religion, it is described that in the past, they used to donate gold coins; that is the equivalent of money, isn't it?

Dadashri: Yes, the donation of gold coins used to take place, but they were donated only to a specific type of people. They were not given to all people. The donation of gold coins was given to certain *Brahmins* (those of the highest social rank in the Hindu caste system, who were traditionally priests and scholars) who subsisted on alms, to those who had some obstacle in getting their daughters married. Secondly, it was given to them for the maintenance of their worldly life. Otherwise, gold coins were not donated to other people. Only those who are involved in worldly interactions and subsist on alms should receive that. The *Brahmins* who subsisted on alms could not ask from anyone. In those days, money was spent for good purposes. This is not the case these days. Even temples of the Lord are being built using 'black' money [money earned through the black market, on which income and other taxes have not been paid]. That is certainly the effect of this era of the time cycle!

From the Perspective of the Gnani...

Questioner: Of all the different types donations, including the donation of knowledge and the donation of money, which is the best according to your view? A dilemma often arises between the two.

Dadashri: The donation of knowledge is considered

the best. Those who have the money, they should give the donation of knowledge; they should give money for *gnandaan*. *Gnandaan* means to publish books or to do other such things. How can knowledge be propagated? Money should be spent only towards this cause. Those who have money should give towards this cause and those who don't should make use of *abhaydaan*. You should behave in such a careful manner that no one becomes frightened by you. It is considered *abhaydaan* when no one is hurt by you nor is afraid of you.

With regard to donation, people [generally] give so that they can be recognized for it and that is not right. They construct memorial walls so that donors' names can be hung on a plaque, but those memorials don't last long. And when does one's giving in this life carry forward [to the next]? When we do something that helps to propagate knowledge, then it will come with us.

The Book That Helps Is Worth It

Questioner: Hundreds of thousands of religious books get printed, but no one reads them.

Dadashri: That is true. What you are saying is true. No one reads them. The books are merely lying around. The book that gets read is of use. What you are saying is true. These days, no one reads books. People keep printing nothing but religious books. What does that *Maharaj* (a high-ranking Jain monk) say? Publish it in my name. So the *Maharaj* inserts his name [for publicity]. He inserts the name of his guru's guru, 'Our guru was like this, and our guru's guru and his guru…. The prestige extends that far back.' People want to be famous and they publish religious books for this reason. Religious books should be such that the knowledge is useful to us, if it is such a book, then it is useful to people. Such a book is worth printing; otherwise, what is the point of printing books just for the sake of it?

And no one reads them either. People put them aside after simply reading them once. No one reads them again, nor does anyone read them in their entirety even the first time. If you have published a book that is helpful to people, then your money will have been spent worthwhile. Moreover, it can be published only if one has the merit karma and if the money has been earned through lawful means, otherwise it cannot be published, can it? It wouldn't be possible, would it! Money will come and go, and credit will never refrain from becoming debit. How does the law work at your end? Does only credit take place or is there some debit as well?

Questioner: There is both.

Dadashri: So credit and debit will always keep on happening.

Questioner: That is indeed what should happen.

Dadashri: But there are two ways. Debit can either go towards a good cause or go down the gutter, but it will go in one of the two ways. All of Mumbai's money is indeed going down the gutter. All the money is indeed going down the gutter.

Mumbai Is Like a Fairground of People With Tremendous Merit Karma

Questioner: The highest amounts of donations take place solely in Mumbai. Hundreds of thousands and tens of millions of rupees are donated.

Dadashri: Yes, but all those donations are for earning recognition and there are also some other good things. There are good things like giving *aushadhdaan*. So, there are many other things in Mumbai.

Questioner: Do the donors get the benefit of these donations or not?

Dadashri: They get a lot of benefit. They would not forgo the benefits, would they! But how much money is there in Mumbai?! In comparison, how many hospitals are there? There is an abundance of money in Mumbai, it is as great as the ocean, and it indeed goes into the ocean!

Questioner: Why is it that all the money accumulates only in Mumbai?

Dadashri: Does money accumulate only in Mumbai? It is indeed the rule that the best of things get drawn into Mumbai.

Questioner: Is that a characteristic of the location?

Dadashri: Definitely of the location! The best of things get drawn into Mumbai. Even the best chili peppers and even prominent people are found in Mumbai alone. And the worst of people, the most unworthy people, are also found in Mumbai. Both the qualities are present in Mumbai. So if you go looking for them in the villages, you will not find them.

Questioner: People in Mumbai are unbiased, aren't they?

Dadashri: It is a fairground of people with tremendous merit karma. It is a kind of fairground filled with people having tremendous merit karma. And all those with tremendous merit karma get drawn here together.

The people of Mumbai accept and tolerate everything. They do not retaliate or do any such thing. If someone steps on a person's foot, the person from Mumbai will keep saying, "Please...." He will not slap the person, but he will keep saying, "Please...." Whereas in the villages, they strike back. So, the people of Mumbai are considered to be developed.

The Money Is Going Down the Gutter!

People's money is indeed going down the gutter; only the money of the rare person who has tremendous merit karma is used for a good cause! Does money go down the gutter?

Questioner: That is what is happening, isn't it!

Dadashri: A large amount of money, money by the truckload has gone down the gutters in Mumbai. It is nothing but a market filled with illusory attachment! One's money is swept away very quickly. The money has been earned through illicit means, hasn't it! It is not money earned through lawful means; if it were lawful, then it would be used for a good cause.

Currently, the entire world's money is going down the gutter. They have widened the pipes of the gutters; why is that? It is because the wealth needs space to flow, doesn't it? All the money that is earned is being wasted in eating and drinking, so it is going down the gutter. Not a single rupee is being spent on the right path and those who are spending the money in giving donation to colleges and other places, that is all egoism! When the money is used without egoism, it is considered correct. Otherwise, one will always find means to feed his ego, he keeps getting fame! But after getting fame, he will get the result of it. Then when that fame turns around, what happens? There is disgrace. Problems arise at that time; instead, you should not have the desire for fame at all. If you have the desire for fame, then disgrace will follow, won't it? Would the one who does not have a desire for fame ever be disgraced?

Use It for a Good Cause

Money may go away and may even fill up at short notice. Do not wait to use it for a good cause. It should be used for a good cause; otherwise, people's money will go down the gutter. In Mumbai, tens of millions of rupees have gone down the gutter. When it is used for purposes related to one's own home and family and not used for others, all that goes down the gutter. So they are now repenting. When I tell them that it has gone down the gutter, they say, "Yes, that is exactly what has happened." So then mortal one, why weren't you cautious from the beginning?! Now when it comes again, be cautious. To which he says, "Yes, I will not be careless again." It will definitely come again, won't it! Money has its ups and downs. Sometimes, there may be two years that are rough, and then the next five years may be great; it carries on like this. But when it is used for a good cause, it will be beneficial, won't it? Only that much is ours, the rest goes to waste.

You earned so much, but where did it go? It has gone down the gutter!! [When one is asked,] "Have you donated to charity?" Then he will reply, "I am not able to make that much money. I am unable to save up, so how can I donate?" So where has your money gone? In this case, who is doing the 'farming' and who is doing the 'eating'? Money does not belong to the person who earns it. It belongs to the person who uses it. So however many new 'overdrafts' [merit karma bound in this life, which will carry forward into the next life] you send, that much is yours. If you did not send them, then the onus is on you!

Donation Means to Plant and Then Harvest

Questioner: There is no relationship between the Self and donation, so then is it necessary to give donations or not?

Dadashri: What does donation mean? It means to give and then take in return. This world is in the form of echoes. So whatever you do, there will be an echo of that, along with its interest. So you give and take in return. You had given in the past life; you had done something such as spending money for a good cause, so you have gotten the result of that. Now, if you don't do such a thing again, then everything will go to ruin. You may have harvested twenty tons of wheat from your farm, but if you do not keep aside five for the purpose of replanting, then what would happen?!

Questioner: Then nothing would grow.

Dadashri: That is how all this is. So you must give, then it will create an echo and return multifold. You had given in the past, that is why you have been able to immigrate to America. Otherwise, is it easy to immigrate to America?! It is when so much merit karma has been bound that one gets to sit in a plane. There are so many people who have never even seen a plane!

Wealth Indeed Comes Back There

Your family was wealthy before, wasn't it?

Questioner: All that is due to merit karma bound in the past life!

Dadashri: It is when others have been helped to a great extent that money comes to you, otherwise money will not come! Money does not come to the one who has the desire to snatch it. If it does come, it goes away, it does not remain. Money does not come to the one who wants to take it by any means possible. Money only comes to those who are desirous of giving. Money comes to the one who expends himself, who gets cheated, who expresses nobility. It may appear to have been expended, but it will return once again.

Make Sure You Don't Miss Out on Donating

It is only possible to give it when it comes, isn't it!

And when a person does not have anything, do you know what he thinks? 'When I get [the money], I will give it away.' And when it comes, he puts the envelope [containing the money] aside [for safekeeping]! Otherwise, the nature of the human mind is such that [one thinks,] 'I will donate; I have one hundred and fifty thousand right now, when I have two hundred thousand, I will donate then.' In this way, it remains pending! When it comes to a matter like this one, it is best to close your eyes and go ahead and give it away.

Questioner: For the person who simply keeps saying, "When I get two hundred thousand, I will donate money," what if he ends up passing away without doing so?

Dadashri: He passes away and the donation is not given. It is not given and nothing is achieved. That is the nature of human beings. Yet, when he does not have [money] he says, "As soon as I get it, I will donate it right away. As soon as I get it, I want to donate it." Now, when it does come, this illusory attachment (*maya*) perplexes him.

Right now, if someone did not return sixty thousand rupees, then he will say, "It is fine now, it must be some karmic account of mine, it was not in my destiny." He will let go of it in that case, but he will not let go of it here [for donation]. The nature of human beings is such that illusory attachment perplexes them. It is only if he is bold enough, that he can give. That is why we say, "Do something," then he will not be perplexed by illusory attachment. If you cannot give a flower, then give a petal. Everyone needs to give someone some support according to their capability, even if it is just one finger's worth. Would a sick person have any problem with simply giving a bit of support with the hand?

A True Philanthropist

That which is never in shortage is called wealth! Even

after you magnanimously keep giving to charity, if there is still no shortage, that is known as wealth. As it is, when a person gives to charity, he gives for two days out of the entire year; that cannot be considered as wealth at all. There was a wealthy businessman who was a philanthropist. Now why was he called a philanthropist? It was because for the last seven generations, the family had kept donating money. He donated magnanimously. He gave donations to whosoever that came. If a person were to show up today, saying, "I want to get my daughter married," then he would give to that person. If some *Brahmin* came, then he would give to him. If someone needed two thousand rupees, then he would give that to him. He had a place built for ascetics and saints to sit and have meals; so he was donating extensively, that is why he was called a philanthropist! 'We' had witnessed all of this. As he would give to each person, his wealth kept increasing.

What is the nature of money? If a donation is ever given for a good cause, then it will increase without limits. That is the nature of money. And if you pickpocket, then no wealth will remain in your home. If we bring all these businessmen together and ask them, "How are you, dear fellow? You must have two thousand rupees in the bank, mustn't you?" Then they will respond, "Sir, I have earned one hundred thousand rupees in twelve months, but I don't have any savings." That is why they came up with the saying that a thief's mother cries with her head in an empty drum [in which grains are stored]! There is nothing inside the drum, so she is bound to cry, isn't she!

The correct way to channel money is through donation, and a true donor is naturally an expert. Upon seeing a person, he will immediately be able to recognize, 'This person seems a bit dodgy.' So he will tell him, "Dear fellow, I will not be able to give you cash for your daughter's wedding.

Whatever attire and anything else that you need, you can come take it from here." And he will tell him, "Bring your daughter over." Then he will give her the attire, jewelry, and all other things. He will send sweets to the relatives from his own place. He follows through with the worldly interactions very well, but he understands that this person is dubious. It is not wise to give him cash in hand. So, even donors are experts.

To Whom Should You Donate Money?

You may give money to an impoverished person but when you examine further, you find that he already has seventy-five thousand rupees. This is because those people are collecting money in the name of being poor. This is all indeed a business that carries on. Where should you donate? You should donate to those who are not asking for it and are feeling oppressed within, the ones who are living under pressure, the common people. These people are feeling very trapped, the middle class!

Donate With Understanding

Knowledge arose in the mind of one person. What knowledge arose? That, 'People must be dying from the cold. I cannot withstand the cold indoors. It is getting ready to snow, so what will happen to those who are living on the streets?' Such knowledge arose for him; this is considered one type of knowledge, isn't it! The knowledge arose and his circumstances were favorable. He had money in the bank, so he purchased a hundred to one hundred and twenty-five blankets of cheap quality! And the next day at dawn, he went to where those people were sleeping and covered them with the blankets. Then when he returned to that place five to seven days later, not a single blanket was in sight. Those people made money by selling off all the new blankets.

So, what I am saying is, you cannot give like this. How could you give like this? You can buy old blankets from the secondhand store and give those to them. No one would bother buying those blankets from them. If you have planned a budget of seventy rupees per person, then instead of buying one blanket for seventy rupees, buy three old blankets if they are available and give the person three blankets. He can cover himself with three blankets; he will not find anyone to buy them.

So, in the current era of the time cycle, give a donation after a lot of forethought. The money [of this era of the time cycle] is bad by its original nature. Even when giving a donation, you will be able to give only after a great deal of thought. Otherwise, you will not even be able to give a donation. And in the past, there was real money, so wherever you donated, it was indeed true donation.

These days, you should not donate cash money, you can get food from some place and distribute it. If you have bought sweets, then distribute the sweets. If you give a package of sweets, then he [the person you give it to] might tell someone else, "I will sell this to you at half the price." Now what can you do to this world? You can get *chevdo* (Indian snack mix), puffed rice. And you can get fritters, break them into small pieces and give those to them, "Here, have this! What is the problem? And take this yogurt, too." They may ask, "Why did you break them like this?" So that they have no suspicion, tell them, "Take this yogurt, you can make *dahivada* (fritters drenched in yogurt)." But what else can you do? There should be some tactic, shouldn't there!

There is no way you can tackle these people, and even if they come soliciting, give them something. But do not give them cash. Otherwise, all of this is getting misused. This only happens in our country. No one in the entire world can solve this Indian puzzle!

If we were to tell someone to solve this puzzle by asking him, "How does this work, what is this? Where did the blankets that were donated go? Conduct an investigation on this." Then he will say, "Call upon the CID [Crime Investigation Department]." Hey, this is not a task for the CID. We will solve this without the CID. This puzzle is an Indian puzzle. You cannot solve it. In your country, you catch people with the help of the CID. We know what people in our country do! Go to the trader's place the next day.

So when will one have the prosperity of money? There should be some law or ethics. It should be there to a more or less extent, shouldn't it! The current era of the time cycle is a bit strange. So, there should be some basic ethics, shouldn't there! Can it carry on like this?

They sell off everything, they even sell their own daughters; they have even sold their own daughters for money. They have even gone this far! Hey, this is not right.

You should not give cash in donation. You can help with his maintenance. You can get him started in a business. If you give money to a violent person, he will commit more violence.

Donate, But With Awareness

You should never be preoccupied with the thought that your money will get used up. At whatever time, however much money is spent, that is correct. That is why it has been said that money should be spent, because in doing so, greed decreases and consequently, one will be able to give frequently.

[Donating with] Applied awareness (*upayog*) is awareness (*jagruti*). When we do auspicious deeds, when we donate, what should the donation be like? It should be one with the awareness that people benefit spiritually. Give anonymously, so as to ensure that you do not get fame or recognition. That is considered as giving with awareness, isn't it! That is considered [auspicious] applied awareness. In the other case, if one's name is not printed [on a plaque], then he will not give again.

Even on the auspicious (*shubha*) path, when is it considered as [donating with] awareness? It is only if it is auspicious, if it is in such a way that it is beneficial in this life as well as the next life; that is when it is considered as [donating with] awareness. Otherwise, a person may be making a donation or serving others, but his awareness does not extend beyond this. If every activity is carried out with awareness, then it will be beneficial for the next life. Otherwise, all of it is being done in a 'sleeping state'. When he gives a donation, he does so while 'sleeping'! Even if a donation of four pennies is given with awareness, that is more than enough! When a person gives a donation with the desire of gaining fame and recognition in return, he does so in the state of 'sleep'. The one who gives a donation for the benefit of his future life is considered 'awake'. Awareness of benefit and harm means that the awareness remains on what is beneficial and what is harmful to the Self! There is no telling what his next life will be like, yet he gives donations in this life, then how can he be considered 'awake'?!

This Is How Obstacles Are Created

If this man is giving a donation to someone, and a person with excessive intellect says, "Hey, why are you giving to this person?" Then this man will say, "Oh, let me give it to him, he is poor." He gives the money in this way and the man who is needy takes it. However, that person with excessive intellect has created an obstacle for himself by saying what he said. So then even when he is in a time of need, he will not find anyone to help him out.

And wherever he creates obstacles, it is indeed there that the obstacle comes into play.

Questioner: What if the obstacles were not formed through speech, but they were created through the mind [by having negative thoughts]?

Dadashri: Obstacles created through the mind will have a greater effect. They will give an effect in the next life, whereas [the obstacles created through] this speech that was spoken will give an effect in this life. When it is done through speech, it is instant, like cash. So its result will also be instant, whereas that which is created through the mind will come into concrete existence in the next life.

And This Is How Obstacles Are Destroyed

Questioner: This means that one should maintain awareness to the extent that a negative thought does not arise.

Dadashri: That is not possible. Such thoughts are not going to refrain from arising. Our job is to erase them. When you decide that such thoughts should not arise, that is known as *nishchay* (firm resolve). However, [to expect] that such a thought should not arise at all, that will not happen. The thought will arise, but you should erase it before it is 'bound' [set in stone]. You may have the thought, 'This person should not be given a donation.' But as You have been given *Gnan* (Knowledge of the Self), the awakened awareness will arise, 'Why did I create an obstacle in this?' Consequently, you erase it. If you erase it before putting the letter in the mailbox, then there is no problem. However, no one can erase it without *Gnan*, can they! A person without Self-realization cannot erase it, can he?! On the contrary, if you tell him, "Why did you have a negative thought like this?" Then he will respond, "I had to. You would not understand." So then he doubles it in that way and reinforces it. The ego does everything that is crazy;

that which causes damage is referred to as the ego. One keeps shooting his own foot; that is referred to as the ego.

Now you can erase everything by repenting, and decide internally, 'I should not speak like this. And I ask for forgiveness for speaking like this.' Then it will be erased. This is because before the letter is dropped in the mailbox, you are making the change. 'Earlier, I had the thought that a donation should not be given. That thought is wrong. However, I now think that it is good to give a donation.' So the previous negative thought gets erased.

To give donations, to oblige others, to maintain an obliging nature, to serve others, all of that is considered relative religion. Merit karma is bound through that. And by hurling abuses, by engaging in physical fighting, by looting, demerit karma is bound. Where there is merit and demerit karma, Real religion does not exist whatsoever. 'Real' religion is free from merit and demerit karma.

A Fifth Portion Is for Others

Questioner: What should be done in this life to bind merit karma for the next life?

Dadashri: However much money you receive in this life, give one-fifth of it to God by donating to a temple, or else use it for the purpose of giving happiness to others. Hence, that much 'overdraft' will reach there! You are enjoying the 'overdrafts' from the previous life. Merit karma bound in this life will carry forward [to the next life]. The earnings of this life will be of use in the next life.

The Custom of Giving Only to God

When I go to visit the Marwadi people [a highly successful business community originating from the state of Rajasthan, India], I ask them, "How is the business?" They reply, "The business is running well." I ask, "Is there any profit?" They reply, "There is a profit of two to four hundred thousand rupees!" I ask, "Do you donate money to temples?" They reply, "We give twenty to twenty-five percent of our profit annually." Is there anything left to say to them? It is only if you sow the seeds in the farm that the grains will grow, isn't it! How can you obtain grains without sowing the seeds? If you don't sow the seeds at all! This is indeed a custom of the Marwadi people, to give donation for a religious purpose. They give for *gnandaan*, for a religious purpose, they give donations at two to three other places, and not for those other purposes, such as giving to high schools or other things, they don't give there; they only give for the former purposes.

Should One Donate to Temples or to the Poor?

Questioner: We had gone to visit the temples; people spend tens of millions of rupees for the stone [from which the idol is carved]. And the Lord has said that a living, breathing God is present within every living being. And people berate these living beings. They make people plead, and on the other hand, they spend tens of millions of rupees on stone idols, why is that so?

Dadashri: Yes, but they make people plead because of their lack of understanding, isn't it! They make people plead because of their weakness of anger, pride, deceit, and greed, isn't it!

The fact is, people go out to earn money. Now, a person may have enough money to run the home, but he still goes out to earn money. So would we not understand that he is setting out to take in what is beyond his quota?! Everyone has the same quota in the world. But these greedy people take an additional quota and some other people do not even get their share. Now, even in this case, they do not get it by fluke, they get it through their merit karma.

If you have bound more merit karma, then you will get money, and then you end up spending that money. You know that this has started to accumulate. When you spend it, it gets deducted, doesn't it? The merit karma certainly accumulates. But you should know how to deduct [spend] it, shouldn't you?

Thus, what people are doing in connection to temples is correct. They want solutions. Where do they want to do *darshan* (devotional viewing)? They want to do *darshan* where they do not feel embarrassed. They feel embarrassed in front of a living person, whereas one will even dance in front of an idol if you tell him to. He dances and jumps around [in a state of devotion] all by himself! However, he feels ashamed in doing so in front of a living person. This [idol] is not living and he cannot do anything in front of a living person. And if one were to do this in front of a living person, then he would attain salvation, he would attain absolute salvation, he would attain ultimate salvation. However, he does not have the capability, does he! He does not have such merit karma!

Whatever one offers to God is not without the expectation of a reward, it is with the expectation of a reward. 'Oh Lord, grant a son to my son! May my son pass [his exams]. The old man at home is paralyzed, may he get cured.' He gives a donation of two hundred and one rupees for this. Now, who is going to give that here [in Dadashri's *satsang*: company or association of those who promote the attainment of the Self]? Do we have such a factory? And who here is going to accept it even if a person does give it?

Even That Is Indeed Violence

Questioner: When a businessman is inclined towards making an illicit profit, when some industrialist or businessman gives less remuneration in proportion to the labor or if income is made without putting in any effort [adulteration of goods, selling short], is that considered an act of violence?

Dadashri: That is all indeed an act of violence.

Questioner: Now, having made money without any effort, if he uses the money to give to charity, then what kind of violence is that considered?

Dadashri: However much is used towards charity, however much he gives up, he incurs that much less of a liability. However much he had earned, if he earned a hundred thousand rupees, and then he built a hospital worth eighty thousand rupees, then he is not responsible for that amount. He is responsible for only the twenty thousand rupees. So, it is a good thing, it is not wrong.

Questioner: People hoard wealth; is that considered violence or not?

Dadashri: It is indeed considered violence. To hoard is violence. It is not useful to other people, is it!

It Goes the Way It Came...

All this is being done in the name of God, in the name of the religion!

Questioner: The person giving the donation believes, 'I have given it upon having faith in the person.' But how are we to know what the person who receives it is going to do with it?

Dadashri: But it is only if your money is earned the wrong way, that it will be used in the wrong way. However much money there is that is earned illicitly, it will be used in the wrong way, and money earned through lawful means will be used in a good way!

Stealing Large Amounts and Making Token Donations

Questioner: Many people say that if one donates, then he becomes a celestial being [in the next life], is that true?

Dadashri: There are even those who go to hell [in the next life] despite donating money. This is because they donate due to someone pressuring them to do so. In fact, in this *Dushamkaal* (the current era of the time cycle characterized predominantly by misery, and almost no happiness), people do not even have the money to give for donation. The money that is present in *Dushamkaal* is money gained by doing terrible deeds. So, on the contrary, when that money is donated, it causes harm. Nevertheless, if you give it to some person who is suffering, rather than giving it for the sake of donation, if you give it to remove his difficulties, then that is good. What is the point of giving donations for the sake of gaining fame? Give food to someone who is hungry; give clothes to a person who does not have clothes. Otherwise, in this era of the time cycle, where can you get the money for donation? There, the best thing is that there is no need to give donation. Have positive thoughts. Where can you get the money for donation? Real money has not come, has it! Nor does real money remain as a surplus. Those who give large amounts of donations, it is money that comes in off the books, it is money under the table. Nevertheless, for those who are giving donations, it is not wrong. This is because one obtains it through the wrong means, but he uses it in the right way, so at least he becomes free from the demerit karma! He planted a seed in the farm, so it grew, so he receives that much fruit!

Questioner: There is a verse in a spiritual composition, 'The smugglers are trying to get released [from karma] by making a token donation.' (*Daanchori karnarao soydaane chhootva mathe.*) So, on the one hand, one engages in smuggling, and on the other hand, they give donations, so they at least gained that much, didn't they? Can we say that?

Dadashri: No, we cannot say that they made a gain. That is a sign of going to hell [in the next life]. That is an unscrupulous intent. The smuggler engaged in stealing and gave a token donation; instead, it would be better that he does not donate any money and straightens up. It's like this, it is better to receive a punishment of a jail sentence for six months; what is the point in being allowed to visit a garden for two days in the middle of the sentence?

What this [verse] is trying to convey is that a person took part in the black market, in smuggling, then he donates fifty thousand rupees so that his name does not get besmirched, so that his reputation does not get ruined, that is why he is giving a donation. This is referred to as making a token donation.

Questioner: So there are no virtuous people these days, are there?

Dadashri: You can't expect a person to be completely virtuous, can you! But this is for those high-profile people who earn tens of millions of rupees and then donate a hundred thousand rupees. Why do they do that? So that their reputation is not tarnished. It is only in this era of the time cycle that the practice of giving token donations is ongoing. This is really worth understanding. Of the other people who give donations, there are some who are householders, their financial condition is average; there is no problem with such people giving a donation. On the contrary, those people [earning through unscrupulous means] give a token donation so that their reputation is not tarnished, they put up a false front to cover up their own reputation! They give donations only for the sake of showing others!!

Currently, are they donating money or taking it away?! And whatever donation is given [using money acquired through smuggling] is a violation of MISA [India's Maintenance of Internal Security Act].

That Money Binds Merit Karma

Questioner: Is it not acceptable to donate 'black' money?

Dadashri: Donation of 'black' money is not acceptable. Nevertheless, if a person is starving and someone gives him 'black' money, then that person may use that money to buy food! And there is a legal problem with 'black' money, but there is no other issue. If that money is used for payment in a restaurant, then would they accept it or not?

Questioner: They would accept it.

Dadashri: Yes, so the cycle continues.

Questioner: Nowadays, 'black' money is being used towards religion, so is merit karma actually earned through such an act?

Dadashri: It definitely is! One has given that much away, hasn't he! He has given away that which came to him, hasn't he! So based on the motive, the merit karma accordingly becomes that way, with that motive! The fact that he donated such money is not the only thing that is taken into account. It is indisputable that he gave away the money. Aside from that, where has the money come from, what is the motive, once all these calculations are made, whatever is left over, that much belongs to him. And what was his motive? 'The government will snatch it away, so why not dump it here instead!'

Give Bountifully, Without Expectations

Questioner: So what if 'black' money is being used, it still gets tagged under the name of religion, that it has been spent for a religious purpose.

Dadashri: Yes, but it is good if it is spent for a religious purpose. Although he does that with the 'black' money, 'black' money is not a big offence. 'Black' money means the tax that the government levies is cumbersome to people. It is much more than what they are willing to pay, so people hide the money.

Questioner: A person who donates with the expectation of getting something in return, even that is not banned in the scriptures. It is not criticized.

Dadashri: It is best if he does not expect anything in return. When he expects something in return, that donation gets cancelled out, it is considered worthless. What I am saying is, give just five rupees, but give it without expecting anything in return.

That Is Like a Camouflage

Questioner: Does 'black' money cause problems wherever it goes or not?

Dadashri: It does not help completely. It comes to our home too, but how much of it? Ten to fifteen percent, not more than that.

Questioner: Does it not help in religious purposes, does it not help as much wherever it is used?

Dadashri: It does not help. It helps in appearance, but it does not take long for it to depart. They are all war quality structures. All the structures are built of war quality! You have seen them, haven't you! They are all camouflaged. Why should you become happy with camouflage?

The Gradual Deterioration of People of the Highest Quality

In the earlier times, there were great philanthropists. Those great philanthropists would come to be when there was unity of mind, speech, and body. And the Lord had referred to them as *shreshthi* (a person of the highest quality). These days, they refer to those *shreshthi* as *Shetty* [a surname or last name] in Chennai. It gradually became distorted from *shreshthi* to *Shetty* over there, and over here [in Gujarat], it has gradually become distorted to *Sheth* [a surname or last name].

I was once talking to a secretary of a mill owner. I asked him, "When will the *sheth* (boss) return? He has gone out of town?" He said, "It will take four to five days." Then he told me, "Listen to what I have to say." I replied, "Sure." He said, "It is worth getting rid of the 'e' and changing it to an 'a' [*sheth* (boss) to *shath* (swindler)]." I explained to him, "Do not say anything as long as you are dependent on the salary paid by him." Otherwise, when you change the vowels, what remains?

Questioner: *Shath* (swindler) remains.

Dadashri: But you cannot say that! This is the state that has come about. There was the great *Jagdusha* [a thirteenth century Jain merchant and renowned philanthropist from Gujarat] and other wealthy merchants! They were referred to as *shethiya* (respected, wealthy merchant).

The Result Is According to the Intent

Many people do not want to give donation, they do not want to give it in their minds, yet they say, "I want to donate," and they do it too, they make the donation. However, because they do not want to give it internally, it bears no fruit.

Questioner: Dada, why does this happen?

Dadashri: One person gives in his mind, he does not have the means to give, and he says, "I want to give, but I am not able to." He will get the result of that in his next life. This is because that is as good as giving. The Lord has accepted that. He at least receives half of the benefit.

A person went to a Jain temple and gave only one rupee, whereas another man who is a wealthy businessman gave a thousand rupee note to the temple. Looking at that, you have the thought, 'Oh, if I had the means, then I would have given.' So, that gets credited for you. You cannot give because you don't have the means. Over here, the value is not of giving, the value is of the intent (*bhaav*). This is the Science of the *vitaraag* (absolutely detached) Lords.

And for the one who donates, what he has may multiply many times over. But what is that like? For the one who wants to give with unity in the mind, speech, and conduct, for him, there will be no end to the result he receives in this world! These days, everyone says, "I had to give because of a particular person, otherwise I would not have given. I had to give because that influential person pressured me to give." So in that case, that is indeed what gets credited too. When you give inwardly, willfully, then it is of use. Do people give because they feel pressured by someone?

Questioner: Yes, yes.

Dadashri: Oh, some donate to maintain their glory, to make a name for themselves, to increase their prestige. Internally, they feel, 'It is not worth giving, but it will look bad if we don't,' so the result will be like that. One gets the result according to the intent he had internally. And if there is a person who does not have [the money to give], and he says, "If I had it, then I would have given it," then what kind of result will he receive?

Gross Karma: Subtle Karma

A wealthy businessman donated fifty thousand rupees. His friend asked him, "Why did you give away so much money?" The businessman replied, "I am not inclined to donate even a single rupee. I had to give it because of pressure from the mayor." Now what will be the result of this? The donation of fifty thousand rupees is gross discharging karma; the businessman receives the result of that right here. People praise him, applaud him, meanwhile what has the businessman charged within, as subtle karma? 'I am not inclined to donate even a single rupee.' He will get the result of that in his next life. So in his next life, the businessman will not be able to donate even a single rupee. Now, who would be able to understand such a subtle point?

Suppose there is another person who is impoverished. The very same people [those who had sought a donation from the wealthy businessman] pay him a visit to collect a donation. So the impoverished person says, "I have only five rupees right now, take all of it. But if I had five hundred thousand rupees right now, I would have given all of it!" He says this from the heart. Now, this person gave only five rupees, this is the result of the discharging of his karma. But what did he charge subtly? To give five hundred thousand rupees; so in his next life, he will be able to give five hundred thousand rupees, when it [the subtle karma charged] discharges.

Suppose there is a person who keeps giving donations, he is very devout and pious [on the outside], he gives donations to temples, he practices *dharma* the entire day, so the people of the world will regard him as a religious person. Now, internally, if that person has thoughts such as, 'How can I accumulate money and how can I enjoy it!' He has a massive desire to take money that is not rightfully his. He is ready to engage in illicit sexual relations!

Therefore, God does not credit even a single rupee of his. What is the reason for that? The reason is that all that [he does externally] is gross discharging karma and he will get the result of that gross discharging karma over here [in this life]. People believe this gross discharging karma to be the karma for the next life. However, one receives the result of that over here itself, whereas the subtle karma is being bound internally, and people do not know about this. One receives the result of that in the next life!

If a person has stolen today, that act of stealing is gross discharging karma. He receives the result of that in this life. For example, he becomes disgraced, the police officers beat him up; he receives all those results right over here [in this life].

Charging Karma to Receive Money

Questioner: Everyone is chasing after money. So that would lead to greater charging, wouldn't it? So they should get more money in the next life, shouldn't they?

Dadashri: If you have charged, 'I want to spend money for *dharma* (giving happiness to others; maintaining good intentions; rightful action),' and do so, then you will receive more [in the next life].

Questioner: But if he keeps maintaining the intent internally that, 'May I attain money,' then as a result of maintaining such an intent, he charges karma, so will nature not provide him with money in his next life?

Dadashri: No, no. Wealth is not acquired through that. If a person maintains the intent to acquire money, then he will not even receive whatever money he was meant to receive. On the contrary, obstacles get created. Wealth is not acquired by thinking about it; it is acquired by binding merit karma.

'Charge' means that one must charge merit karma in order to acquire wealth. Moreover, one will not receive money alone. While charging merit karma, if he has the desire for money because he feels he has a big need for it, then he will acquire money. Someone else may say, "I only want religion." Then he will receive religion alone, and he may even not have any money. So you fill the tender of merit karma, that, 'I want this.' In acquiring it, merit karma gets used. Someone may say, "I want bungalows, cars, I want this, I want that." So the merit karma gets used up in that. He will have nothing left over for religion. And someone else may say, "I only want religion. I do not want cars. Even if I have two rooms of this size, it will do, but I primarily want religion." Then he will have more of religion and less of other things. So based on that merit karma, he fills the tender once again.

With Such Intents, the Donation Is Useless!

When you think of it, don't you feel that this Science of the *vitaraag* Lords is so magnificent that it makes you liberated?! It is indeed so magnificent! If you realize this, then gather the understanding from the *Gnani Purush* (One who has realized the Self and is able to do the same for others) and have your intellect become *samyak* (that which takes one towards the Real), then you will be able to progress [spiritually]. Even in worldly interactions, people get their intellect to become *samyak* through me. Even if they have not taken *Gnan*, if they sit with me for some time, then their intellect becomes *samyak* and they can progress! What would be one's plight without this *Gnan*? If a person understands this, then it is of use!

Questioner: Without attaining *Gnan*, this is such that it will never come to an end.

Dadashri: This is such that it will never come to an

end. It is not even worth discussing it. Even if a person is giving a donation of fifty thousand rupees, what does he tell you? "I am donating because there is pressure from this prominent businessman, I wouldn't otherwise." It is not enough that he alone knows about it, but he lets you know as well. And he informs others too, "I am so shrewd a person." You see all this happening out there in the world, don't you? It [the donation] unnecessarily goes to waste. Therefore, for those who remain in *satsang*, their work is done, isn't it! The troubles of the entire world are done away with, aren't they!

Donate, but Anonymously!

Questioner: For the one who is concerned only with attaining the Self, fame should have no bearing, should it?

Dadashri: Fame is a very harmful thing. When one is on the way to attain the Self, his fame will spread widely, but he has no interest in that fame. The fame will indeed spread, won't it! Upon looking at a sparkling diamond, everyone will say, "It is shining so brightly, it has so many facets." People do say such things, but one himself doesn't find enjoyment in it. Whereas in matters of fame in worldly life, people are indeed beggars for fame. There is beggary for fame and that is why one donates a hundred thousand rupees to a high school, or to a hospital, but as he gets recognition for it, that's more than enough for him!

Moreover, in worldly interactions, they say to keep the donation anonymous. Now, only a rare person donates anonymously. Everyone else donates because they have beggary for fame. People give them praise, "Kudos to this businessman! He gave a donation of one hundred thousand rupees!" And so he gets the reward [of the donation given] here itself [in this life].

So upon giving, he received its reward right here. And for the one who maintained anonymity, he kept the reward for the next life. The reward will inevitably be handed out. Whether you accept it or not, there is definitely a reward for that.

Donation is to be given according to one's own desire. The rest is all fine; it is a part of worldly interaction. Someone may put pressure on you to donate. Someone else may give a person a garland of flowers, so then he donates.

Donation should be anonymous. The way these Marwadi people donate money to temples privately! When no one knows about it, it yields result.

That Worldly Interaction Is Considered Good

Questioner: You spent money [towards a good cause] after Hirabaa was gone, what is that considered in worldly interaction?

Dadashri: That is considered good in interactions of worldly life.

Questioner: We indeed have to align with the interactions of worldly life.

Dadashri: That is indeed the case in interactions of worldly life, but this looks good in worldly interactions. But I don't do things to look good. It was because Hirabaa had the desire that I did so. I do not care about looking good or bad, nevertheless, 'we' live in such a way that it doesn't look bad.

Questioner: That is about you, but what about us?

Dadashri: You have to conduct yourself [in accordance with worldly interaction], don't become too insistent, but conduct yourself in a normal way.

Merit Karma Is Expended in Seeking Praise

Questioner: If the law is as you are saying, then whatever you spent [towards a good cause] after Hirabaa was gone, you will receive merit karma for that.

Dadashri: What will I get? I have nothing to do with it. I do not have anything to do with it at all, do I! Merit karma is not bound this way. On the contrary, merit karma gets expended in this, when people give praise.

Or else, if someone does something bad, then people will say, "Just look at the fool, he ruined everything." So everything gets used up here and now. When a high school was built, praise was received here and now. There is nothing to gain later [in the next life].

Questioner: The school was built for the children, they received an education, it led to an inculcation of good thoughts.

Dadashri: That is a different thing. However, when people sing your praises, that is it. It has been used up.

Can Someone Receive on Behalf of Someone Else?

Questioner: The praise goes to the one for whom the money has been spent, not to us. Whatever deed we do for a person, the result of that goes to him. Whatever good deed we do for a person, he gets the result of it. We do not receive it. The one who does it does not get it.

Dadashri: We do it and the other person gets it? Have you ever heard of such a thing?

Questioner: We are doing it on behalf of that person, aren't we?

Dadashri: Doing it on someone's behalf?! What would be the problem if you were to eat on his behalf? No, no.

That is no different. People actually fool others and guide them down the wrong track, by saying that it is on behalf of someone! If we were to eat [on his behalf] since he is not eating, then is there anything wrong with that? Everything in this entire world is governed by law!

The Energies of the Self Blossom There

Besides, that [which is done for the Self] will come along [in the next life]. This will not come along. You get the reward here immediately; you receive praise immediately. And what is saved for the Self will come along.

Questioner: What did you say will come along?

Dadashri: It is what you give there, for the Self; so, the energy of the Self blossoms a lot. And that comes along with You.

Questioner: And whatever is spent here, one gets only praises for that, doesn't he?

Dadashri: He got that. He got the praises.

The Feast of Praises

Questioner: When I give a donation, my intent is for a religious cause, for a good cause. But when people praise me for that, does it all not get cancelled out?

Dadashri: When a person gives big donations, it becomes revealed to all and everyone sings his praises. And there are other donations as well that no one knows about and so no one sings praises and therefore, they yield benefits! You should not get into this hassle. You do not have the intent internally that people 'feed' you [with praises]! There should be only this much intent! The world even sang praises of Lord Mahavir! But He Himself would not accept them, would He? People sing praises even of this Dada! But He Himself does not accept those, does He! Whereas these hungry people accept them immediately. They cannot refrain from disclosing that they gave a donation. People do not refrain from singing praises, but if you don't accept them, then what is the problem? The 'disease' will seep in only if you accept them, isn't it?! The one who doesn't accept the praises has no problem. He doesn't accept the praises, so he doesn't incur any loss. And the one who praises binds merit karma. Merit karma is bound by supporting good actions. So this is how everything works covertly. These are all laws of nature.

For the one who sings praises, that is beneficial for him. Moreover, for those who listen, the seeds of good intent are implanted within them, [they feel,] 'This is worth doing, we didn't even know about this!'

Questioner: We do good deeds through our body, mind, and wealth, but what should be done if someone only says negative things about us and insults us?

Dadashri: The one who is insulting you is binding immense demerit karma. Now, in this process, your karma gets washed away and the one insulting you becomes a *nimit* (an apparent doer who is simply instrumental in the process).

Love for Praise

Oh, I would evaluate my nature! I used to go to [the Shrimad Rajchandra Ashram in] Agas. At that time, I was a contractor by profession. Now, I had a hundred rupees to spare; money was very valuable at that time, but I still had enough money to spare. When I would go to Agas, I would put down some money for a donation. I would take out a hundred rupee note and tell them, "Take twenty-five rupees and give me seventy-five rupees back." Now, it would have been fine if I did not take back the seventy-five rupees. But the mind was stingy and miserly, so I would take back seventy-five rupees.

Questioner: Dada, even at that time, you would observe so minutely?

Dadashri: Yes, but what I am saying is that this nature, the *prakruti* (inherent characteristic traits) doesn't leave, does it! So then I examined within. As such, people would tell me, "You are very noble!" I wondered, 'How is this noble?!' I am being stingy here. Then, upon examining, I discovered that I would spend one hundred thousand rupees where I would get praised, otherwise I would not give even a rupee. That nature was not completely stingy. But where there would be no praise, be it a religious organization or anything else, I would not give, and if they praised me, then I would give all my earnings. I would do this even by incurring a debt. Now, how long do the praises last? Three days. There is nothing afterwards. It is remembered for three days and after that, there is nothing.

See, I remember this. I would give a hundred rupees and take back seventy-five rupees. I can still See that. I can See that office. But I said [to myself], 'What kind of behavior is this!' How broad-minded these people are! I had understood my pattern of behavior, my pattern of behavior in its entirety. In a way, I was broad-minded too. However, I would need people who would praise me and flatter me. If they would flatter me, then it would work.

Questioner: Dada, that is the nature of a living being.

Dadashri: Yes, that is the *prakruti*, that is all the *prakruti*.

Moreover, this person, the one [a *Vaniya*: the caste that merchants, money-lenders, and traders belonged to in the traditional Indian caste system] sitting there, he is shrewd. He does not get cheated by praises. [He evaluates,] 'Does this get credited for the future or does it finish here itself?' Where praises are received, this [the merit karma] gets used up. I took its fruit, I tasted it, whereas this person does not seek praises, he looks for the fruit there [in the next life] as an 'overdraft'; they are very shrewd, astute people, are they not! They are more astute than us. We, the *Kshatriyas* (the warrior caste), don't overthink, we just get on with it! All the *Tirthankar* Lords (the absolutely enlightened Lords who can liberate others) were *Kshatriyas* too. The monks themselves say, "We cannot become a *Tirthankar*. This is because when we become a monk, we renounce a lot of things, but we still hide and keep one gold coin! What if difficulties arise someday?" That is their main tuber, whereas you [a *Kshatriya*] would renounce everything immediately. Promise to pay means nothing but a promise! You do not know anything else, do you? There is no other understanding within. You are not a thinker at all. But they [the *Vaniya*] get liberated earlier.

Questioner: They get liberated earlier!

Dadashri: Yes, those people attain liberation. They attain absolute Knowledge (*keval Gnan*). However, only the *Kshatriyas* can be *Tirthankars*. The *Kshatriyas* all acknowledge that to me that, "We are considered *Kshatriya*. We do not know all such things [that the *Vaniyas* know]. They are very profound [thinkers]." And they are astute people! They think everything through, they put in a lot of forethought before taking action. And for *Kshatriyas*, there is no end to repenting. Whereas they have less to repent over.

...But It Got Wasted in a Donor Plaque

Suppose a person donates a hundred thousand rupees to charity and his name gets engraved on a donor plaque. Whereas another person gives only one rupee to charity, but he gives it anonymously; then this anonymous donation is of great value, even if only one rupee is donated. And to get a donor plaque placed means the balance sheet has been settled. If you give me a hundred rupee note, and I give you [a hundred rupees worth of] change, then there is nothing left for me to take, nor is there anything left for you to give! You gave to charity and had your name engraved on a donor plaque, so no further exchange remains, does it! This is because you gave to charity, and in exchange, a donor plaque was placed. Whereas for a person who donates only one rupee in private, he hasn't taken anything in return, therefore his balance is pending.

'We' have visited temples and the like. At some places, entire walls are covered with donor plaques, they are strewn with donor plaques! What is the value of those donor plaques? It is for the purpose of recognition! And where there is an excessive amount for the purpose of recognition, people do not even bother looking at them. They think, 'Why is this worth reading?' If there is only one donor plaque in the entire temple, then one will have the time to read it, but here there is an excessive amount, entire walls upon walls are covered with donor plaques, so what would happen? Nevertheless, people say, "Put a donor plaque in my name!" People only like donor plaques, don't they!

One Gave Money and Accepted the Donor Plaque

Questioner: Some people give without understanding, so there is no point in that.

Dadashri: No, they do not give without understanding. They are very shrewd. They indeed do what is beneficial to them.

Questioner: Without understanding *dharma*, they give for recognition, they give so that a donor plaque is placed.

Dadashri: In terms of recognition, it is only recently

that it has become for the purpose of recognition! In the past, it was not for recognition. Only recently have they started selling their name, because of this *Kaliyug* (current era of the time cycle, which is characterized by lack of unity in thought, speech, and action; also known as *Dushamkaal*). Otherwise, in the past, there was nothing like this for recognition. They would keep giving all the time, so what would the Lord call them? The Lord referred to them as *shreshthi* (person of the highest quality). And these days, they are referred to as *Sheth* (successful businessman or owner; also a surname).

Keep Maintaining Auspicious Inner Intents

Questioner: On the one hand, I have the intent that I want to give everything for donation, but that does not actually end up happening.

Dadashri: You are not likely to give like that! Is it easy to give? To give donation is a difficult thing! Nonetheless, maintain the intent. To give money towards a good cause is not under your control. You can have the intent [of giving], but you may not be able to give. And you will get the result of that intent in the next life. How can a 'spinning top' give a donation? And when he gives it, it is *vyavasthit* (the result of scientific circumstantial evidences) that makes him do so, that is why he gives. A person gives donation because *vyavasthit* makes him do so. And a person does not give donation because *vyavasthit* does not make him donate. The *vitaraag* Lords do not have illusory attachment (*moha*) for taking or giving donation. They are *shuddha upayogi* (Those with pure applied awareness of the Self)!

At the time of giving a donation, if the intent arises that, 'I am making a donation,' the *parmanu* (the smallest, most indivisible and indestructible particle of inanimate matter) of merit karma get drawn in. And while doing wrongful deeds, the *parmanu* of demerit karma get drawn in. Later, at the time of giving the result, it gives either a pleasant result or an unpleasant result. As long as one has ignorance of the Self (*agnani*), he suffers the result, he suffers pleasure and pain. Whereas a *Gnani* does not suffer that, He continues to Know it.

What Is Good Use of Money?

Questioner: Suppose due to merit karma, someone has accumulated hundreds of thousands of rupees, then should he distribute it to people who are impoverished or should he use it for himself?

Dadashri: No, he should use that money in such a way that the family members do not become unhappy. He should ask the family members, "You don't have any [financial] difficulty, do you?" If they reply, "No, we do not," then that is his limit to use the money. So then he should do so accordingly.

Questioner: It should be used for a good cause, shouldn't it?

Dadashri: All money should be used for a good cause. Money used for the home will all go down the gutter. So, when it is used in other places, it creates a 'safe-side' [safeguard; safety] for you yourself. Yes, you can't take it with you from here [into the next life], but you can create a 'safe-side' in another way.

Questioner: But in a way, that can be considered the same as taking it with you, isn't it!

Dadashri: Yes, it is indeed like taking it with you, for your 'safe-side'. So, use it in a way that it gives happiness to others. All of that is your 'safe-side'.

Questioner: What is considered good use of money?

Dadashri: When you use it for the benefit of people or for God, that is considered good use of money.

Even 'Our' Intent Remained All the Time

If I had the money, then I would have donated money too, but no such money has come to me yet, and if it does come, then I am still ready to give it. It's not as though I am going to take everything with me! But give something to others! Nonetheless, instead of giving money to the world, I show them a path as to how they can become happy in the world and how they can live their life. As far as money is concerned, if you give a person ten thousand rupees, then the next day, he will quit his job. Money should not be given like this. To give money in this way is an offence. It makes a person lazy. That is why a father should not give too much money to his son; otherwise, the son will become an alcoholic. If a person gets the opportunity to take it easy, then that's it, he goes down the wrong track!

Should a Person Give Money to His Children or Donate It?

Questioner: Due to the unfolding of merit karma, what if we get more money than we need?

Dadashri: Then you should spend it. Do not save too much for your children. Educate them, complete everything for them, help them get a job, so then they will start working. So do not keep aside too much for them. Keep some money in the bank, ten to twenty thousand rupees, so if he ever encounters hardship, then you can give it to him. Don't tell him that you have kept the money aside. Yes, otherwise, even if he does not have any difficulty, he will get into a difficulty.

One man asked me, "Should I not give anything to my children?" I replied, "Give to your children; whatever your father gave you, give all of that to them. Everything earned in the interim is yours. Give it to charity wherever you find suitable."

Questioner: Even according to the governmental law, ancestral property must be passed down to the children, whereas the father can do anything with the money that he earns of his own accord.

Dadashri: Yes, he can do whatever he wants to. You should indeed do it yourself! What our path says is that whatever is yours, keep that money separately and use it [towards a good cause], then that will come with you. This is because after taking this *Gnan*, you have one to two lives remaining, so you need to take something with you, don't you! When you go out of town, you take some food with you, so wouldn't you need all of this?

Questioner: Can it be considered better when one remains as a trustee?

Dadashri: It is best to remain as a trustee. But one cannot remain like that, not everyone can remain like that. Moreover, one cannot remain as a trustee completely. A trustee means he oversees with detachment. But he cannot completely remain as a trustee. However, if he has such an intent, then he can remain as that to a certain degree.

And how much should you give to your children? Whatever your father had given to you. Even if he did not give you anything, you should at least give something.

Do children ever become alcoholics, if they have plenty of wealth?

Questioner: Yes, they do. We should not give them to the extent that they become alcoholics, but we should at least give them something, shouldn't we?

Dadashri: Only a limited amount should be given.

Questioner: If we give more wealth, then that can end up happening.

Dadashri: Yes, that will always be harmful for him towards attaining liberation. It is always better if it is done within limits. It is an offence to give more to your children. All the foreigners understand this! How wise they are!! Whereas these [Indians] have greed that extends to seven generations! 'The children of my seventh generation should have this.' How greedy these people are! It is your duty to help your sons begin earning, that is your duty, and you should get your daughters married. You should give something to your daughters. These days, they give a share to the daughters as partners, don't they? Expense is incurred when you get them married, isn't it? And in addition to that, you should give them a certain amount. You give her jewelry, you certainly give her that, don't you! However, you should indeed spend what is yours.

Questioner: We should give our sons a house, a business, and some money on loan, shouldn't we?

Dadashri: If you have a million dollars or even half a million dollars, then you should buy your son the house in which he lives. Then, help him set up a business, one that he likes. Ask him what business he likes and then help him set up the business he likes. And help him get twenty-five thousand to thirty thousand from the bank as a loan. Let him keep paying off that loan and you should give him a certain amount too. You should give him half the amount he needs and the other half as a loan from the bank, so he keeps repaying the loan. Meaning, you need someone to keep him on his toes, so that he does not start drinking alcohol. Then, if your son says, "This year, I am unable to repay the loan." Then tell him, "I can lend you five thousand, but you should give it back soon." So you should lend him five thousand. Later, remind him of that five thousand. "I have told you that you need to return that amount soon." When you give him a reminder like this, he will say, "Don't nag me right now." So you should understand that this is very good. It means that he will not come to borrow money again, will he! You shouldn't have a problem with him saying, "Don't nag me." At least he will not come to borrow again, will he!

So, not only do you maintain your 'safe-side' but you also do not look bad in front of your son. Your son will say, "My father is good, but my nature is not straightforward. That is why I said negative things. But my father is very good!" So escape and run away from this world [in this way].

The Ideal Will

Give the daughter a certain proportion. Give to the son, but only a certain proportion. You should retain half of the capital. That means private! It means you should not declare it. You can declare everything else and tell them, "The two of us will need that as long as we are living, won't we?"

So you should deal with this systematically, with the proper understanding.

Questioner: But what should the will be like after the death of the person?

Dadashri: No, not after death; whatever amount you have, if you have a capital of two hundred and fifty thousand rupees, then don't keep it until you die. As far as possible, make an 'overdraft'. Make an 'overdraft' by giving towards hospitals, for *gnandaan*, and everything like that and then give your children whatever remains. You should even increase that amount a little. They [the children] have insatiable greed, so to satisfy that insatiable greed, set aside fifty thousand. Then convert the rest of the two hundred thousand rupees into an 'overdraft'; what will you do with the money in your next life? At present, you are using all the 'overdrafts' from the past life, so won't you have to make an 'overdraft' in this life? Yes, you have not given this to anyone. When it is used for the benefit of others, for the salvation of others, that is considered an 'overdraft'. Those who have given solely to their children have regretted it, they have regretted it immensely! You should understand what to do for your children's own good. You should come and discuss this with me.

That is why I say that instead of the money going to waste, do something so that it is used for a good cause. It will be of use to you in the next life, whereas when you leave from here, they will tie four coconuts [to the bier, as per Hindu custom], won't they! Moreover, your son will say, "Give me the cheaper ones, the ones without any water!" If you have surplus money, then use it for a good cause, use it for the happiness of others. Only that much is yours, the rest goes down the gutter…!

Such things should not be spoken. Yet 'we' are saying them!

Settle the Accounts Like This

Questioner: Say there is a person to whom we have lent five hundred rupees and he is not able to return it. And secondly, we have donated five hundred rupees. So what is the difference between the two?

Dadashri: To give a donation is a different thing. In the second case, the one who accepts the donation does not become a debtor. You are reimbursed for your donation in some other way. The one who accepts your donation does not give you anything in return. Whereas in the other case, the person whom you lent the money is the very person through whom it will be returned. Eventually, even if it is in the form of a dowry, he will return the money to you.

Don't people in our culture say, "The boy comes from a poor family, but his family is very noble. So, give him fifty thousand rupees in dowry!" Why are they giving this dowry? This is in fact the money he was owed that was not repaid. So all the accounts are like this. Not only does give away his daughter, but he also gives money. So all the accounts are being settled in this way.

A Trustworthy Advisor

If someone snatches five thousand dollars from your hand, then what would you do?

Questioner: It has been snatched many times like that. All the property has been lost as well.

Dadashri: What do you do then? Doesn't anything arise in the mind?

Questioner: No, nothing.

Dadashri: That is good; in that case, you are wise. Money indeed comes to get snatched. If it cannot get used here, then it will get used there. Therefore, put it to good use; otherwise, it is bound to get used in other places. This is the nature of money, so if it does not get used in the proper way, then it will get used in the wrong way. Some of it gets used in the proper way, and most of it gets used in the wrong way.

Questioner: Show me the right way. How can I know whether it is the right way or the wrong way?

Dadashri: In terms of the right way...'we' do not accept a single rupee. I wear clothes paid by my own money. I am not the owner of this body! I have not been the owner of this body for the past twenty-six years. I am not the owner of this speech. Now, when you have some confidence in me, when you place some trust in me, then I can tell you, "Give your money to a certain place, then it will be used for a good cause." When you have developed some confidence in me, and I tell you this, then will there be a problem with that?

Questioner: No.

Dadashri: That indeed is the proper way. What else? The advisor should be trustworthy. One you can trust! One who does not take even the slightest commission! When there is not even a penny of commission, that is when he is considered trustworthy! 'We' have not come across anyone trustworthy like that. 'We' have come across those who take a commission indiscriminately....

Questioner: Dada, please continue showing us the way.

Dadashri: Wherever there is any commission, the money gets used the wrong way! Up until now, not even four *annas* (a former Indian currency unit that is equivalent to 1/16th of a rupee) of this spiritual organization has been spent towards hiring a clerk! Everyone finishes the work with their own money, this is how this spiritual organization is, a pure organization! So, this is the right way. Give whenever you wish to give, and moreover, do so if you have the money, otherwise, do not give it. Now, if this person asks, "Can I give again, Dada?" Then I would say, "No. Keep operating your business." He already gave once! There is no need to give again over here! If you have the money, then give according to your capacity! If you have the capacity to lift ten pounds, then lift eight pounds, do not lift eighteen pounds. This is not to be done for the purpose of becoming unhappy! However, 'we' show this way so that the surplus money does not get used the wrong way. Otherwise, the *chit* (inner component of knowledge and vision) remains and moves around only in greed! That is why the *Gnani Purush* shows you that you should give at a certain place.

Donate Money to Temples of Simandhar Swami

If you have extra money, then there is nothing better than donating it to a temple of Simandhar Swami [the absolutely enlightened living Lord, through whom it is possible to attain final liberation]. And if you have less money, then there is nothing better than to feed *mahatmas* (Self-realized Ones in *Akram Vignan*)! And if you have even less money than that, then give to someone who is in need. That too, do not give cash, send them food, drinks and other such things! Despite having less money, you can afford to give donation, can't you?

Recognize Simandhar Swami

You have heard of Simandhar Swami, haven't you? 'He' is currently a *Tirthankar* (an absolutely enlightened Lord who can liberate others) in *Mahavideh Kshetra* (one of the three locations in the universe where humans reside)! 'He' is present today.

How old must Simandhar Swami be, sixty or seventy? 'He' is one hundred and seventy-five thousand years old! 'He' is going to live for yet another one hundred and twenty-five thousand years! I am establishing a link, a connection with Him for you. This is because that is your destination. One more lifetime still remains. Final liberation (*moksha*) will not happen directly from here. One more lifetime still remains. You are going to be sitting with Him; that is why I am establishing a connection for you.

And this Lord will bring salvation to the entire world. The entire world will attain salvation! The entire world will attain salvation through Him as a *nimit* (active evidence)! This is because He is living. 'Those' who have already attained final liberation can do nothing for you; only merit karma gets bound [by worshipping Them].

Give Donation Where There Is Exclusive Devotion

We want to go to *moksha*; we require enough merit karma to go to *moksha*. However much you do [worship, devotion, donation] for Simandhar Swami over here, all of that gets accumulated. That is more than enough. It's not that this is less. Give however much you have decided to, do all of that; with that, everything gets encompassed. Then, there is no need to do any more than this. Then, if you build hospitals or something else, that falls under a different direction. That too is merit karma unfolding, but it is *paapanubandhi punya* (karmic effect of merit karma of this life, which binds demerit karma for the next life), it makes you bind demerit karma. Whereas this [whatever you do for Simandhar Swami] is *punyanubandhi punya* (karmic effect of merit karma in this life, which binds merit karma for the next life).

They Are Akin to Living and Awakened Gods

What is the most suitable use of money today? One might ask, "Is it to give donations outside? To give money to colleges?" No, to feed our *mahatmas*. To give them satisfaction is the best approach. *Mahatmas* like these cannot be found anywhere in the world. There [where *mahatmas* are present], *Satyug* (era of the time cycle that is characterized by unity in thoughts, speech, and action) is indeed evident. And if you visit them, their only desire the entire day is of how good things can happen to you.

If you don't have the money, then you can eat or stay at [some *mahatma's* place], all that is indeed ours. It is mutual. Whoever has surplus [money], use it. And if you have an abundance [of money], then use it to give happiness to all human beings, that is good, and beyond that, use it for the happiness of every living being.

Otherwise, if you give to schools and colleges, you

will get recognition for that, but this is genuine. I give you a guarantee that these *mahatmas* are completely genuine. It doesn't matter what they are like. They may have less money, yet their motives are clean, moreover, they have very good intentions. The *prakruti* (inherent characteristic traits) is bound to be different for each individual. These *mahatmas* are akin to living and awakened Gods. The Self has manifested within them. They do not forget the Self even for a moment. The Self has manifested within them; God is present there.

Questioner: Do we not get the result of feeding people?

Dadashri: You do get the result of it, but you get praised for it here itself, that is all. You get the result of that here itself. Whereas you get the result of that [donation] for which you are not praised over there [in the next life].

Questioner: So one has to take it [the merit karma bound as a result of giving a donation] along with him, isn't that so?

Dadashri: You have to take that with you. The [merit karma bound as a result of giving] ten rupees, you have to take that with you, and if you get praised over here, then it has gotten used up.

Questioner: In that case, we will have to stop feeding people from tomorrow.

Dadashri: Feeding people is mandatory for you. There is no choice but to carry out that which is mandatory.

What is this like? You should feed *mahatmas*; it is a different thing to feed other people. You will get praised for that. Here, no one has come to praise you. You will never find such *mahatmas* nor will you find any *Brahmins* who are like them in this world. They do not have any desire to take anything from you, these *mahatmas* do not have any ulterior motive. What are these *mahatmas* like? They do not get involved in taking any sort of advantage. So where would you find such *mahatmas*?! The entire world is selfish; these *mahatmas* are genuine people. There cannot be such people anywhere in this world!

They [*mahatmas*] do not have the ulterior motive that this doctor will come in handy someday. Such a thought never even arises in their mind, whereas for those people [without Self-realization] when a doctor shows up, they immediately think, 'He will come in handy someday.' Hey mortal one, why are you doing this, for the sake of obtaining medicine?! You are healthy, yet you are running around for the sake of obtaining medicine.

If only one understands a word of what I say about these *mahatmas*; they are like God, but these *mahatmas* are not aware of it. If you serve them tea, serve them a meal, serve them some other food, that is considered the greatest *yagna* (a Hindu ritual in which things are offered into a sacrificial fire with a specific objective), it is a first class *yagna*. Even if one sells their bangles to feed them, it is very good. Bangles do not give peace. If one sits with *mahatmas*, they do not have any deceitful intent. So, you should keep feeding *mahatmas* as much as you can. Even if you serve them a cup of tea, it is more than enough.

Such Understanding Needs to be Given

One man was asking for my advice; he asked, "I want to give donation, so how should I give it?" So I thought, 'This person does not have the understanding about giving money.' I asked him, "Do you have money?" To which he replied, "Yes." So I said, "Give it in this way." I know that this person has a very pure heart and he is guileless, so he needs the right understanding.

What had happened was that 'we' had gone to visit

someone. He sent a driver to drop me off, specially to drop me off. That [pure-hearted and guileless] man told the doctor, "Don't take Dada back in the car. I will drop him off." So, he came to drop me off and we ended up having a conversation! He was asking me for advice, "I want to donate money, but where should I give it, how should I give it?" [I said,] "When you built the bungalow, you must have made money." He replied, "I built a bungalow, I built a cinema. Just recently, I donated one hundred and twenty-five thousand rupees in my town." So I told him, "If you have earned a lot of money, then get an *Aptavani* [a series of fourteen volumes compiled from Dadashri's speech] printed." He immediately replied, "Your wish is my command. I did not know this. No one gives me such understanding." Then he said, "I will get it printed immediately, within this month." Then he asked me, "How much will it cost?" To which I replied, "It will cost twenty thousand rupees." He immediately replied, "I will get these many books printed!" I told him not to rush into it.

So if there is a guileless person like this who does not understand about giving donations, and if he asks, then 'we' show him the way. 'We' know that this person is guileless. If he doesn't understand, 'we' show him. Otherwise, there is no need for 'us' to tell those who have the understanding, is there! Otherwise, they will feel hurt. And 'we' don't want to hurt them. 'We' do not have any need for money at all. Donate only if you have surplus. This is because there is no donation like *gnandaan* in the world!

When someone reads the books of this Knowledge [of Dadashri's], so much change takes place within him. So donate money if you have it; if you don't have it, there is no need at all for it over here!

Donate Only What Is Surplus

Questioner: What is considered surplus?

Dadashri: As far as a surplus is concerned, if you donate today and it leads to some worries tomorrow, then it is not considered surplus. If you feel that you will not have any trouble for six months, then you can donate, otherwise do not do so.

However, if you do this [create an 'overdraft' by donating towards Simandhar Swami], then you will not have to face any trouble. This work will get completed on its own. This is the work of the Lord. Those who do this, their earnings automatically remain level. Nevertheless, I have to caution you. Why should I tell you to give blindly? Why would I ask you to do such a thing blindly? I am only cautioning you for your own good that, 'It is because you had given in the past life that you are getting these things in the current life. And if you give in this very life, then you will receive again [in the next]. This is indeed your own 'overdraft'. I have nothing to do with it. I am guiding you to give to a good place, that is all. You had given in your past life and you are reaping that in this life. Is it as though everyone is not intelligent? The answer is, you did not receive it on account of intelligence. It has indeed carried forward from the past! If you had credited an 'overdraft' in the bank, then you will get the cheque in your hand. Moreover, if the intellect is good [inclined towards donating], then the money is again channelized towards donation.

Such Subtle Understanding Even While Accepting Donation

Here, the only expense is for the books that are being printed, and there is that much confidence that the money for the books will indeed come automatically. There are active evidences (*nimit*) behind that and they will all come together. 'We' do not need to shout or beg. If 'we' ask someone for it, then he may feel hurt. He will say, "Such a large sum?" When he says, "Such a large sum," it means he feels hurt. So we get confirmation of that, don't we? And if someone feels hurt, 'we' have not remained in 'our' *dharma* (moral duty). Thus, 'we' cannot ask in the least. If he says it willingly, then 'we' take the money. 'We' can only accept it if he understands *gnandaan*. So all those who have donated, they have done so after understanding *gnandaan*. They have donated of their own accord. To this day, 'we' have not asked anyone for it.

Your money is used in a commendable way when you have books printed here, and this can only happen if you have the merit karma. They can only be printed if the money has been earned through lawful means, otherwise, they cannot be printed. It would not work out, would it!

There Is No Competition Here

And nor is there any need to reveal it for the sake of competition. There is no place for competition here, things like who has made the highest pledge, 'This person has pledged this amount and this other person has pledged this much!' There is no such competition as far as the *vitaraag* Lords are concerned. However, this has become commonplace in the current era of the time cycle. These are the signs of *Dushamkaal*. To compete like this is a grave disease. People get involved in interactions characterized by animosity. Here, there are no such characteristics. Money is not solicited here.

Talk From the Bottom of Dada's Heart

There is such an overwhelming number of letters that come from people and it is difficult to address all of them. There will be others who will take care of the printing. 'We' will distribute these [books] free of cost the first time around. Thereafter, people will take care of printing additional ones of their own accord. Right now, it is important that this *Gnan* that has manifested does not become forgotten. That is why it must be put in print. And later on, someone or another will inevitably come along and voluntarily take on the responsibility [of additional printing]. There is nothing that is mandatory here. 'We' do not have any laws over here. 'No law' is the law.

Bliss Upon Letting Go of That Which Is Dear to You

When will one attain *samadhi* (a blissful state that comes about when one becomes free from mental, physical, and externally induced suffering)? It is when one relinquishes that which is most dear to him in the world. What is the thing that is held most dear in the world? It is money. So relinquish it. Someone told me, "Once the money was relinquished, more of it started coming in." To which I replied, "If more of it comes in, then relinquish more of it." If you relinquish that which is dear to you, *samadhi* arises.

The Path of Liberation Is Like This

This person was magnanimously giving away what he had. Then he was asking me, "What is the path to liberation?" I replied, "This is indeed the path to liberation. What other path to liberation can there be besides this? Magnanimously give away what you have for the purpose of liberation. That is considered the path to liberation." Ultimately, you will have to relinquish everything, won't you? Is there anyone who has been able to get by without doing so? What do you think?

Magnanimously give away what you have to others. And that too, for a good purpose, for liberation or for the seekers of liberation, for spiritual aspirants, or for *gnandaan*, magnanimously give away whatever you have. That is indeed the path to liberation.

❖ ❖ ❖ ❖ ❖

Spiritual Glossary

Gujarati Word	English Translation
aahaardaan	donation of food; also known as *annadaan*
abhaydaan	being in a state of conduct which does not induce fear in or hurt any living being
agnani	ignorant of the Self
annadaan	donation of food; also known as *ahaardaan*
aushadhdaan	donation of medicine
bhaav	intent
Brahmin	those of the highest social rank in the Hindu caste system, who were traditionally priests and scholars
chit	inner component of knowledge and vision
daan	donation
darshan	devotional viewing
dharma	giving happiness to others; maintaining good intentions; rightful action; moral duty; religion
Dushamkaal	the current era of the time cycle characterized predominantly by misery, and almost no happiness
Gnan	Knowledge of the Self
gnandaan	donation of knowledge
Gnani	One who has realized the Self and is able to do the same for others

Gnani Purush	One who has realized the Self and is able to do the same for others
Kaliyug	current era of the time cycle, which is characterized by lack of unity in thought, speech, and action; also known as *Dushamkaal*
Kshatriya	the warrior caste
Lakshmiji	the Goddess of wealth; Hindu personification of money
mahatma	Self-realized Ones in *Akram Vignan*
maya	illusory attachment
moha	illusory attachment
moksha	liberation
nimit	an apparent doer who is simply instrumental in the process; active evidence
paap	demerit karma
paapanubandhi punya	karmic effect of merit karma of this life, which binds demerit karma for the next life
parmanu	the smallest, most indivisible and indestructible particle of inanimate matter
prakruti	inherent characteristic traits
punya	merit karma
punyanubandhi punya	karmic effect of merit karma in this life, which binds merit karma for the next life
samadhi	a blissful state that comes about when one becomes free from mental, physical, and externally induced suffering

samyak	that which takes one towards the Real
satsang	company or association of those who promote the attainment of the Self
Sheth	successful businessman or owner; boss; also a surname
shethiya	respected, wealthy merchant
shreshthi	a person of the highest quality
shubha	auspicious
Tirthankar	the absolutely enlightened Lord who can liberate others
upayog	applied awareness
Vaniya	a member of the caste that merchants, money-lenders, and traders belonged to in the traditional Indian caste system
vitaraag Lord	absolutely detached Lord
vyavasthit	result of scientific circumstantial evidences

❖ ❖ ❖ ❖ ❖

Books of Akram Vignan of Dada Bhagwan

1. Adjust Everywhere
2. Anger
3. Aptavani - 1
4. Aptavani - 2
5. Aptavani - 4
6. Aptavani - 5
7. Aptavani - 6
8. Aptavani - 8
9. Aptavani - 9
10. Autobiography of Gnani Purush A.M.Patel
11. Avoid Clashes
12. Brahmacharya: Celibacy Attained With Understanding
13. Death: Before, During and After...
14. Flawless Vision
15. Generation Gap
16. Harmony in Marriage
17. Life Without Conflict
18. Money
19. Noble Use of Money
20. Non-Violence
21. Pratikraman: The Master Key That Resolves All Conflicts (Abridged & Big Volume)
22. Pure Love
23. Right Understanding to Help Others
24. Science of Karma
25. Science of Speech
26. The Current Living Tirthankara Shree Simandhar Swami
27. Simple and Effective Science for Self-Realization
28. The Essence of All Religion
29. The Fault Is of the Sufferer
30. The Guru and the Disciple
31. The Hidden Meaning of Truth and Untruth
32. The Practice of Humanity
33. Trimantra
34. Whatever Has Happened Is Justice
35. Who Am I?
36. Worries

'Dadavani' Magazine is published every month in English

Contacts

Dada Bhagwan Foundation

India :
Adalaj : **Trimandir**, Simandhar City, Ahmedabad-Kalol Highway,
(Main Center) Adalaj, Dist. : Gandhinagar - 382421, Gujarat, India.
Tel : + 91 79 35002100, +91 9328661166-77
Email : info@dadabhagwan.org

Bangalore : +91 95909 79099
Delhi : +91 98100 98564
Kolkata : +91 98300 93230
Mumbai : +91 93235 28901

Other Countries :

Argentina : **Tel:** +54 9 376 4952565
Email: info@dadabhagwan.ar

Australia : **Tel:** +61 402179706
Email: sydney@au.dadabhagwan.org

Brazil : **Tel:** +55 11999828971
Email: info@br.dadabhagwan.org

Germany : **Tel:** +49 700 DADASHRI (32327474)
Email: info@dadabhagwan.de

Kenya : **Tel:** +254 79592 DADA (3232)
Email: info@ke.dadabhagwan.org

New Zealand : **Tel:** +64 21 0376434
Email: info@nz.dadabhagwan.org

Singapore : **Tel:** + 65 91457800
Email: info@sg.dadabhagwan.org

Spain : **Tel:** +34 606245646
Email: info@dadabhagwan.es

UAE : **Tel:** +971 557316937
Email: dubai@ae.dadabhagwan.org

UK : **Tel :** +44 330-111-DADA (3232)
Email : info@uk.dadabhagwan.org

USA-Canada : **Tel :** +1 877-505-DADA (3232)
Email : info@us.dadabhagwan.org

Website : www.dadabhagwan.org